Bride Behind the Boots
PRAYING OVER YOUR FIREFIGHTER

MORGAN LANE

Copyright © 2021 by Morgan Lane
Published by Seaside Lane
Seminole, Florida 33776
www.seasidelane.com
ISBN -978-0-578-86477-8

Library of Congress Cataloging-in-Publication Data
Name: Lane, Morgan author.
Title: Bride behind the boots / Morgan Lane

THE HOLY BIBLE, NEW INTERNATIONAL VERSION®, NIV®
Copyright © 1973, 1978, 1984, 2011 by Biblica, Inc.™ Used by permission.
All rights reserved worldwide.
Cover design by Morgan Lane + Illustration
Illustration by Morgan Lane
Interior & Cover Design by Jodi Costa

All Rights Reserved. No part of this publication may be reproduced, stored in a retrieval system, or transmitted, in any form or by any means, electronic, mechanical, photocopying, recording, or otherwise, without the prior written permission of Seaside Lane.

Printed in the United States of America.

*To my fellow fire wives,
I am grateful to grow with you as we seek more of
Jesus and more for our marriages.*

TABLE OF CONTENTS

Introduction 7
    Heart of Bride Behind the Boots

1. Strength 20
    Give Him the Strength to Save

2. Alert, Aware, & On Guard 30
    Give Him Situational Awareness

3. Quick & Efficient 39
    Give Him an Organized Vision and an Urgency to Help

4. Protection & Safety 48
    Give Him Protection from Danger

5. Fulfilled & Blessed 56
    Give Him Fulfillment in the Work of his Hands

6. Selfless Service 66
    Give Him a Servant's Heart for Christ

7. Divine Peace 76
    Give Him Peace in Surrounding Hurt

8. Godly Courage 88
    Let Him Do the Impossible with God

9. Wisdom & Discernment 98
    Give Him Guidance by the Holy Spirit

10. Love 110
    Give Him Love for His Wife, Family, Department, & Christ

11. Growing 120
    Give Us Minds to Grow

End Notes 125

Acknowledgments 127

About the Author 131

INTRODUCTION

Dear Faithful Fire Wife,

These words are written for you to be an anthem of love, motivation, and a tool. Use them how God leads you. Each chapter contains the following sections:

SCRIPTURE

God's Word is powerful, alive, active, and true.

STORY

You are not alone. Other fire wives and I stand where you are today. I want to share with you hope through my journey and experiences as a fire wife.

PRAYER

A direct connection to the Creator of the universe. A tool to use over your husband's life and your own, to make an eternal impact as you navigate life in the fire service.

FAN INTO FLAME

A challenge to spark you into action. This section of each chapter is inspired by 2 Timothy 1:6, "For this reason I remind you to fan into flame the gift of God." Just as you fan a campfire with more oxygen to produce a vast flame, I want you to fan intentional love into your marriage, producing a flame of great strength. Hopefully, growing the fire of love between you two, that will be full of commitment and passion.

ARTWORK

I have hand-painted these fire wife scripture and quote cards just for you. They are designed in such a way to be torn out or cut out and hung up! You can fill your home with little reminders to pray for your husband throughout your day.

JOURNAL

A blank space for you to date, journal, doodle, or pour out your thoughts. This could be a great place to jot down a list of ideas on how you will personally respond to the *Fan into Flame* challenges.

OUR MEN ARE *selfless* IN THEIR SERVICE TO OTHERS, MAY WE BE *persistent* IN OUR PRAYERS FOR THEM

Bride Behind the Boots

Go in order, chapter by chapter, or flip around to what pertains to you in that moment or season of life. Maybe even join with another fire wife and pray together. Opening these pages with accountability and someone to talk it over with might be the greatest blessing. Allow this book to be a conversation starter to strengthen old friendships or start new ones. Write in the journal section if God tugs you to dive deeper into a verse, topic, or the Fan into Flame challenges that you will soon become familiar with. On your quiet nights at home when he is lying in bed at the firehouse, or more likely running calls, you can use these moments for an eternal purpose, to cover your fireman in prayer. May your heart never grow weary, may you stand strong, and love deep. Our men are selfless in their service to others; may we be persistent in our prayers for them.

Heart of *Bride Behind the Boots*

I was nineteen-years-old sitting in church, just shortly after my high school graduation. My heart was calm and content. My Bible and pen were resting on the lap of my favorite pair of jeans. My short blonde hair just brushed the back of the chair that God had placed me in that morning. My arms were already slightly sun-kissed from my first summer beach days as a high school graduate. The preacher asked that morning, "What is your purpose or calling?" He encouraged us to write a personal thought down on a small note card placed before us at the beginning of the service. The first idea that popped into my bubbling thoughts was, "To honor Jesus and tell others about Him." This was the Sunday school answer that was ingrained into my mind since I was very young. I had taken hold of the concept as my own and fully believed it in my heart. Loving and preaching Jesus had to be the "right" calling to scratch down with my pen. However, my hands wrote a completely different string of words before my mind could even process them, "To be the faithful wife of a firefighter." I can still see the cream color note card resting in my lap on that Sunday morning.

 I was not dating at the time. My heart was young and free, ready for college adventures with Jesus leading the way. I certainly had no intention to tie the knot anytime soon. God hadn't even placed His perfect guy in my life yet. Therefore, the words written before me seemed surprising, yet specific, and straight forward. Once I had met my husband about a month after writing that notecard, I knew that God had a plan much bigger than my nineteen-year-old mind could even dream or imagine!

Only weeks after meeting the man who would become my husband, practically a stranger to me at the time, I woke up in the middle of the night overwhelmed. This is the prayer God led me to declare over him:

"Give him the strength to save. Help him to be alert and aware of all situations and surroundings to bring you glory. Help him to be quick and efficient with calls, patients, and fire. Have him be on guard. Please protect him and give him a fulfilling, safe shift. Help his service to be selfless for you. Give him divine peace through the surrounding hurt and pain. Engulf him with Godly courage to do the impossible through you. Give his heart wisdom and discernment. I pray he can comfort others with love and compassion as you do, Lord. Surround him with guardian angels and fill him with the fire of your Holy Spirit. Protect and bless him, sweet Lord. But most of all, let your will be done."

I had only known him for a few short weeks, however, I felt God push me to share this prayer with him while he was on shift one evening. This is the prayer, my sweet fellow fire wives, that inspired this book. I have this prayer painted on a canvas and it has been hanging on a wall in our home since the day we were married. I read it out loud daily when I pass by it, declaring God's will to be done. As if it is my anthem and duty as a fire wife to declare those statements.

We got engaged just five months after I sent him that prayer. We were married the following year. The decision to become his came as easy as my next breath. However, I knew that the call of my line of duty was high. Just as high as his.

**I am the bride behind the boots,
who has to protect our marriage with
scripture and prayer daily.**

Fighting for the things that really matter. By no means am I a Bible or prayer scholar. I am just a fellow wife and mother who is passionate about the life-changing gift of coming before the Father with an open heart. Keep that in mind as you read.
I am coming from the perspective of being the wife of a firefighter paramedic. Many of my stories are about the EMS side of the service. My husband is also one of the three divemasters in his department. We live in Florida, which happens to be surrounded by water. You will notice me referring to this as well. Know that these prayers are for me and my heart, and my husband and our marriage. Written for me, but also for you. For your heart. For your husband and your marriage. Don't be afraid to mark these pages with a pen, highlight, and rewrite parts in a journal. Make these pages raw, real, tattered, and yours. Write your own prayers by mine, or add in your husband's name specifically to personalize it. I am learning, listening, and loving right along with you in this fire wife life.

I AM THE *bride behind the boots* WHO IS TO *protect* OUR MARRIAGE WITH *scripture* AND *prayer* DAILY

Bride Behind
the Boots

Fellow brides, may this book be a tool, and the Spirit be your guide. Whether your loved one is just starting fire academy, a probie, a seasoned vet, or about to retire from many years of service, may you find hope and encouragement here!

Morgan

The encouragement and conversations on fire wife life don't end here! Join me, Morgan, on Instagram, Facebook, or my website for more thoughts, art, and encouragement.

Instagram @SeasideLane

Facebook.com/SeasideLane

SeasideLane.com

Morgan@SeasideLane.com

Bride Behind the Boots

Chapter One

STRENGTH
GIVE HIM THE STRENGTH TO SAVE

Isaiah 40:29
"He gives strength to the weary and
increases the power of the weak."

Strength for our husbands can mean a handful of things in the fire service. Physically, having to pull a hose, lift someone onto a stretcher, or long hours of overhaul after the fire is out. Mentally, having to remember what they are trained and taught to do for each call, as well as, using their instinct and God-given strength to act in a situation. Spiritually, depending on the Lord, knowing that He is the ultimate giver of strength to get through it all. When my husband had his first ride-along, he was only seventeen-years-old. He was curious to see what the career of a firefighter paramedic was like. He experienced two challenging calls during his first glimpse into the fire service. First, he was face-to-face with a patient, a high schooler, the same age as him, unconscious due to drugs laying on a table before him. It scared him a bit. The other call was a deceased lady. For the first time in his life he watched the words roll off the paramedic's lips, telling the family that their loved one was dead. He had no background with death, making the future seem uneasy. It was a test of fear or faith. The choice to take a step forward or retreat into a more comfortable career choice. Would these calls and this type of job bring too much heartache?

> **Each call is very different.**
> **It is most likely one of the worst days**
> **of that patient's life.**

Shortly after that first ride along, my husband was turning to God for answers. That's when he was reminded of Joshua 1:9, "Have I not commanded you? Be strong and courageous. Do not be afraid; do not be discouraged, for the Lord your God will be with you wherever you go." My husband declared that strength would overpower his fear. To this day, when a call comes in and the details show something serious, as he steps into the engine or rescue vehicle, these are the words that flood back. *Be strong. Be courageous. Be fearless. I have got you, my son, and I will*

Bride Behind the Boots

go before you. God will always be the perfect strength for our husbands to tap into.

I want to talk about physical strength for a moment. This was something that we never had as a family priority until recently, building physical strength as a goal. Last year we moved to a new home. We decided to turn the largest room into a gym, a hard decision at first as I dreamed up a playroom, a homeschool room, or an art studio space. Almost a year later, I can say it was the best decision we ever made. My husband chuckled as he walked behind me in our bathroom mirror as I brushed my teeth one evening. He flexed a tad and said, " I've had multiple people comment to me on how I look built and stronger since the last time they've seen me." We both smiled. I praised him. It was true, we both had been growing in self-discipline physically, which seemed to overflow into self-discipline and healthy habits in so many other areas of our lives. Our bodies belong to God, so we should steward them for His purposes and His glory. That means making fitness and health a priority as a testament to our belief in God.

Moving our bodies can be a form of walking out of our faith. Not to glorify ourselves in our good looking physique, or shaming our body and working out hard to change the features we dislike. Be kind to your body; it is a temple. Find a healthy rhythm for your lifestyle that can reflect God. A simple stretching routine or a walk has been my movement lately. Nothing fancy. I am constantly asking my husband to pray for me to want to move my body, because Jesus gave it to me to steward. Because truthfully, I don't always want to. I pray you will also be an encouragement to your husband, to move his body and be the best he can be in strength: physically, spiritually, and emotionally.

PRAYER

Lord, I pray that you give my husband the strength to save, not by his power, but by yours. Physically would you help him accomplish the tasks that are placed before him today. Give him the desire to stay fit and active, so he can do his job to the best of his ability. I pray he desires to move daily to steward his earthly body well. Keep his mind strong. Help him never to stop learning and growing as a Firefighter/EMT/Medic/Driver/Lt./Captain. Grow his mental strength today through calls, continued education, and peers. If he becomes weary, may he see your hand, God, and be reminded to tap into the mighty power that you have for him in his weakness. Fill his heart with more of you, resulting in an overflow of your strength in every step he takes. Thank you for giving my husband strength today. *Amen*

FAN INTO FLAME

Upon starting this prayer journey for your husband, pick a place of prayer. We have three kids, a dog, and lots of activities on our fire family calendar. I chose my "prayer place" to be wherever I am in my home when I fold laundry. It's a mindless action that I do almost daily, and honestly, I don't particularly enjoy doing it. However, I have wired my brain to always say a prayer over our marriage and my husband when I fold. I meet Jesus when I fold laundry. Your commute to work, sitting at your child's soccer practice, doing dishes, or even brushing your teeth could be your "prayer place". Pick a "place" today that will become a sanctuary of prayer no matter how detailed or simple the prayer might be. Simply meet with the King there and see how the Lord will soften your heart and connect you closer to your husband through consistent prayer.

JOURNAL

Bride Behind the Boots

Chapter Two

ALERT, AWARE, & ON GUARD
GIVE HIM SITUATIONAL AWARENESS

1 Corinthians 16:13-14
"Be on your guard; stand firm in the faith;
be courageous; be strong.
Do everything in love."

Being alert, aware, and on guard may be a difficult task when our men are busy, sleep-deprived, hungry, and ten calls deep on a shift. There are countless situations, both medical and fire, where I want my husband's full attention to be in tune with all the factors going on around him. A rescue call when someone has been wounded by a bullet, I want him to see potential dangers. For a fire that is raging, I want his mind to be clear and able to assess all surrounding factors before going into flames or taking action.

Being alert in our husband's line of duty can protect his life, or another's life.

Being vigilant may mean the difference between life and death. May their hearts also be on guard to the enemy's spiritual attacks while at work.

My husband was on a two-story industrial structure fire and the smoke had risen to the second story making visibility zero. He and his partner were crawling on the hot floorboards of the second floor, feeling with their hands to navigate their way through. As the smoke thickened, they worked their way with a hose line to the heat source. At one point, my husband reached out his hand to find a gaping hole in the floor. He easily could have fallen through it to the first floor. His caution, his partner, and I believe a guardian angel all kept that from happening. Being alert and aware of their surroundings is so important in the fire service. It can either mean coming home safe to us or a tragic accident.

My husband is also a paramedic in a busy area, and the volume of calls he runs in a shift is pretty high. One evening, he had a call for someone who was drunk and under the influence of drugs sitting on a city bench. He was sure, with just a glance, that the enemy had overtaken this patient. The patient was snarling and even threw a punch at my husband. He was just the medic trying

BEING *alert* IN OUR HUSBANDS LINE OF DUTY CAN *protect* THEIR LIFE OR ANOTHERS LIFE

Bride Behind
the Boots

to simply assess vitals and help the patient get to the hospital. In both situations, I thank God that his guard was high, and he was in tune with his surroundings, which in turn kept him safe. Our husband's daily reality is encountering illegal drugs, drunks, arson, beatings, shootings, forest fires, and other frightening situations. Sin and pain are so real in our fallen world. Even if your fireman works in an area that does not have the same diversity of calls, we still must pray for alertness. Our prayers for their presence of mind are critical as the enemy is always looking for ways to dishearten our men.

PRAYER

Lord, I pray my husband will be alert. As calls progress, keep their minds sharp and communications clear in all circumstances. Alert him and his crew of any potential danger upon arriving on the scene. I pray he will be aware. Bring forth any knowledge or perception about a call or patient that can help save my husband or the patient's life. I pray he will be on guard. Help him to protect and defend himself, his crew, and all those he encounters physically. Give him a clear mind empowered by the Holy Spirit to resist the enemies work. May you give him the clarity he needs to do his job well. *Amen*

FAN INTO FLAME

Do one service act this week that increases your husband's alertness at work. Make him breakfast and coffee before shift so he has some extra energy. Let him nap, or take a break from the kids to unwind and prepare for his next shift. Hold his hands and declare a simple prayer of awareness and encouragement over him the night or morning before going to the firehouse. God's great love and your genuine words may be just what he needs to hear to strengthen and give life and alertness to his day.

JOURNAL

Bride Behind the Boots

Chapter Three
QUICK & EFFICIENT
GIVE HIM AN ORGANIZED VISION AND AN URGENCY TO HELP

Isaiah 43:2
"When you pass through the waters, I will be with you; and when you pass through the rivers, they will not sweep over you. When you walk through the fire, you will not be burned; the flames will not set you ablaze."

We live in a house with three toddlers, therefore, we watch toddler cartoons. And, of course, given dad's job title of "firefighter," we watch every kid show that has anything fire-related. One of the common themes in these shows is the speed in which a firefighter can get their gear on and get to the scene. While it might seem like a typical firefighter expectation, I pray that it will always be seen as high importance to my husband.

Seconds can save lives.

Each year our seaside city holds a three-day race car event downtown. My husband works as a member of the fire rescue dive and marine team for the event. They are on call in case a racecar, citizen, or boat needs help from the water. A few years back, I'll never forget, after returning home from a long day in the sun of working this event, I asked him how his day went. He proceeded to explain that he and his crew practiced repeatedly putting on their diver rescue gear. Putting the gear on over and over again, timing each other, and practicing all day so that they could react quickly and efficiently to any water-related emergency. I smiled at him. I prayed that night that he would always have that same desire to be urgent and efficient. Being able to put on his dive gear a few seconds faster could save a person's life in a submerged car or a little child who has fallen off a dock.

Additionally, may their preparations and training at the firehouse be done with focus and care to ensure a fast and efficient response when called on the scene, and to show honor and respect for their crew and patients. May their hearts be reminded of God's faithfulness, like the verse from Isaiah states. From parting the waters of the Red Sea, "When you pass through the waters, I will be with you," to keeping Daniel's three friends safe in the fiery furnace, "When you walk through the fire, you will not be burned." With the knowledge of God's faithfulness in the past

Bride Behind
the Boots

to protect his followers in the most difficult situations, may our husbands walk through fire, knowing they have a faithful God.

PRAYER

Lord, help my fireman to be quick and efficient. Give him an organized vision and an urgency to help others. May he never grow complacent at the tasks placed before him. Bring him back to the vision and reason why he first desired to be in this line of service. Remind him that efficiency and helpfulness are what he was drawn to. I pray that when my husband lacks desire or efficiency in his field of work, that you rekindle his passion for serving others and allow him to be an encouragement to his crew. I also pray that his heart would be released from the pressure and haunting thoughts of a bad call. Protect him from the negative thought of, "If only I was faster, they might still be alive." We know that you are in control of all things. I pray my husband will turn to you when he feels he is too slow. Help him to be sharp and driven today. *Amen*

FAN INTO FLAME

Ask your man how long it takes him to don his gear…he might know how many seconds it takes. Give him a wink and challenge him to be faster today than he was in the past.

JOURNAL

Bride Behind the Boots

Chapter Four

PROTECTION & SAFETY
GIVE HIM PROTECTION FROM DANGER

Psalm 91:11
"For he will command his angels concerning you to guard you in all your ways"

There are only a handful of careers where as you watch that person you love walk out the door, you whisper,

"Come home safe."

Then you watch them drive off, and you mean it with every fiber of your being. When my heart is doused with fear about all the "what if" scenarios that could happen on a shift, I usually have a little chat with God. "Hey, this is out of my control. To quiet my frenzied fire wife mind right now, send an extra angel or two his way. Please and thank you."

Protection and safety is a topic that we seem to chat about often in our household. Every time I'm told an "intense fire story" from his last shift, I always have fear-driven questions that spill out of my mouth. "Did you go in with a partner?" "Did you wear your mask during overhaul, because you know carcinogens?" I don't mean to blurt these things out right away, like a broken fire wife record, but they obviously show my lack of faith in an all-powerful God and trust in my man's judgment.

Another scary place is when I later hear about him responding to an active assailant call. Recently my husband responded to a shooting. He came home and described the gun wound that went right through someone. I will spare the details, but after those calls, my first statement is always, "I'm going to write that letter." It's an ongoing letter I have in my mind that I desire to submit to the city and the fire department. I think each station needs to have a set of bulletproof vests by the turnout gear. If a gunshot wound call comes in, the unit can grab them on their way out. As wives, we could probably write a whole book just on potential fears over our men's safety and wellbeing, but not today. We are going to pray for the protection of Jesus over them instead.

Bride Behind
the Boots

PRAYER

Lord, I release my husband's protection and safety over to you. May you surround him with your guardian angels today and allow him to do his job well for you. Place a hedge of protection around my husband. (Job 1:10) Not a brick wall, but a living hedge that grows thicker and stronger. I desire these prayers for him to be the care, nourishment, and attention that the hedge needs to grow. He encounters others' "worst days" from disease, gunshot, suicide, flames, and so many other things that the enemy intends for evil. May you protect him, physically and spiritually, to bring light into these situations. May you bless and keep him, Lord, for he is yours. *Amen*

FAN INTO FLAME

The opposite of protection and safety is fear and harm. Your challenge today is to take captive those dark trails of thoughts that lead to fear about your husband's job, and replace them with a statement of truth. When our hearts are focused on worship and His Word, there is no room for our fears to spiral out of control. Turn the worry into worship. Express or communicate one of the fears you have out loud with your firefighter or a fellow fire wife. Saying it out loud will help shed light on the insignificance of it in light of the power of Jesus.

JOURNAL

Bride Behind
the Boots

Chapter Five

FULFILLED & BLESSED
GIVE HIM FULFILLMENT IN THE WORK OF HIS HANDS

Psalm 90:17
"May the favor of the Lord our God rest on us; establish the work of our hands for us-- yes, establish the work of our hands."

An occupation in the fire service, EMS, or medical field, in general, can have a lot of constants. However, it can also be like a rollercoaster due to each call being so different. Our men might not feel the glowing emotions of fulfillment and elation when they show up to their job. Burnout sneaks up fast, and the turnover rate for switching to a different career is exceedingly high. Even with Jesus leading us and an incredible marriage, my husband feels worn down in seasons. I've heard many stories of careers cut short as a result of the demanding nature of the job combined with the sinful nature of man.

 I mention the sinful nature of man because we live in a fallen world. Pain and sin will always exist on this side of eternity. We know who has defeated sin, Jesus. Yet living in a job where you witness and feel the effects of the fall of man daily can be pressing, even to a believer. It probably comes as no surprise that the average EMT or paramedic only holds their position for five years (Backberg, 2019). My man is seven years in as a medic, and can feel burnout from tough calls, never sleeping, and cold meals. My prayer is that they cling to the moments when they have peace and affirmation that this is exactly where God wants them to be.

Recently, my husband encountered a first-time experience in his career. The patient was being transported to the hospital experiencing chest pain. The man's heart stopped. He was dead. His partner started CPR, and he placed the defibrillation pads on the patient and shocked him. Suddenly the man lying before him woke up. He could state his name, where he lived, and what year it was. Calls like this reignite his passion and lift his spirit. I thank, praise, and smile when he shares stories like this with me, knowing that it is stuck in his heart as an encouragement. That particular patient even contacted my husband a couple of months later and explained that he had a widow-maker heart attack, and that the hospital was able to clear the blockage to

Bride Behind
the Boots

GOD GIFTED HIM THE HONOR OF BEING THERE TO DO WHAT HE IS TRAINED TO DO ON THIS *earth* AS A MEDIC WHILE WITNESSING A *heavenly miracle*

allow him more time with his family. He saw God bring someone back to life before his very eyes.

God gifted him the honor of doing what he was trained to do on this earth as a medic, while witnessing a heavenly miracle.

The positive moments help him feel fulfilled. However, I also want to pray blessings upon your husband in what may also feel like the mundane. When he is going to that same elderly patient at 6:00pm, and then at midnight, then back again at 3:00am because they have fallen and can't get up. When someone has had a toothache for five days and decides to call 911 in the middle of the night for your husband to pay a visit. Pray for their hearts to feel the reward of those calls, even if on this side of heaven they experience frustration from them and no reward. May God's favor rest upon our men, no matter how big or small calls may seem in earthly terms.

PRAYER

Lord, I pray you bring fulfillment to my husband. May his heart be reminded of all the reasons why he chose this career. Help him find encouragement today through his crew, the rewarding calls, and his desire to work hard for his family. Guide him to take on or even step down from certain aspects of the career in your timing. Promotions and demotions are okay. May you walk with him during each season of life. May he focus on the fact that his diligence and faithfulness to the fire service and God is a testimony to others of hope within the job. Open his eyes to your favor and divinely orchestrate blessings with each patient. Fill him, Jesus, with more of you. More of you first, and the rest will follow. *Amen*

FAN INTO FLAME

Open up a line of hopeful and encouraging communication. Ask your firefighter some of the reasons why he chose this job. Ask him about his favorite call that has encouraged him to keep going.

JOURNAL

Bride Behind
the Boots

Chapter Six

SELFLESS SERVICE
GIVE HIM A SERVANT'S HEART FOR CHRIST

Luke 6:35
"But love your enemies, do good to them,
and lend to them without expecting to
get anything back.
Then your reward will be great,
and you will be children of the Most High,
because he is kind to the ungrateful and wicked."

Being selfless is one of the hardest things. Due to our sinful nature, it is nearly impossible not to think of oneself first. That being said, simple actions reflect a selfless heart and speak volumes to others about Whose you are. You belong to the King as a cherished daughter or son. If your husband is a Christian, then he is washed clean by Jesus and has the perfect example of selfless service to follow. May our men look to Christ as an example of how to serve their department, crew, and patients with a deep love that can only come from Jesus.

You may be thinking, "Girl, I need help. Picking up this book and reading these prayers is out of desperation because I know Jesus, but my firefighter does not. Now, here I sit praying for 'selflessness' in his career when he won't even do a dirty dish at home or acknowledge my 48 hours of keeping the kids and household running." Sweet sister, know that you are seen. Know that our heavenly Father is smiling down on you for making it to this chapter and being diligent for your husband. Pray for his salvation and his selfless service. Continue the good walk of being an example for him as a selfless servant. Take the time to be filled up with the Word of God. I state this line in the introduction of this book: "Our men are selfless in their service to others; may we be persistent in our prayers for them." I truly mean it with all my heart. The most effective way we can serve them is through prayer.

Help him to have open eyes for the needs of others despite his own comfort.

My husband was having a rough shift. A few quick texts came through on my phone about an elderly man who was having trouble breathing. He had a photograph of his newborn

HELP HIM TO HAVE OPEN EYES FOR THE *needs of others* DESPITE HIS OWN COMFORT

Bride Behind
the Boots

granddaughter by his bed with a note saying to show the man the photo to remind him of his granddaughter. Due to the Covid19 virus pandemic, he had to be apart from her. My husband ached for the man who was in great physical pain. He stood gowned, head to toe, in protective virus gear, unable to help much in the situation before him. Just after leaving the elderly man, they got called to a woman who had been in a severe car crash and was trapped in her vehicle. He and his partner were able to get the lady out and on her way to the hospital. That was the last update I had from him. Side note: we don't always communicate this much on his shifts, however, some days need extra prayers. He knows expressing it to me will turn on my intentional prayer heart. What I shared with you was just one of those days.

 I returned to my phone a while later, knowing of his already trying day, and tapped on Facebook. To my surprise, a live news feed video popped up at the top of my screen. There was my husband, pulling on a heavy dry dive suit with long yellow tubes of compressed air floating on top of the pond in front of him. I watched him jump into the deep, mucky, presumably alligator-filled pond to attempt the recovery of someone who had drowned. My eyes welled up with tears. I noticed his muscles and sweet curly hair, making my heart skip a beat. My man is a hunky hero popping up on the news feeds of so many others, as well as my own. My heart was flooded with gratitude for his selfless service. No one else watching the live feed knew what he had been through with the elderly man or the car accident victim just moments earlier. I could only pray a prayer of gratitude. "God, you know his day. I know his day. He is doing his best to serve the community for you. Though he may be exhausted or defeated, his wife has been encouraged to be a bit more selfless herself."

PRAYER

Lord, today may my husband reflect you. You were the ultimate example of a servant. May he walk in humility, considering others before himself. Give him fresh eyes to see others as you see them. If my husband does not already know you, I pray you will soften his heart to see you. Help me to be an example of selfless love for him and my family. Remind us both that each day we have the power to choose our attitude. Even if yesterday was rough, your mercies are new today. Today, help my husband to put others higher than himself. Thank you, God, for your ultimate act of selflessness, going to the cross for us. I pray my husband and I have gospel-driven humility. *Amen*

FAN INTO FLAME

Go on a secret selfless service mission today. Do one, or more if you're really spunky, acts of service for your husband. Make his coffee. Fold his uniforms and stack them up how he prefers them. Tidy up the bathroom or make the bed...so you know it looks nice and inviting for fun activities meant for married couples. I've noticed in my home, when I start the service cycle, it softens his heart and he typically will reciprocate with love. From there, it is just rinse and repeat! Remember, if the service goes unnoticed, your heavenly Father sees your efforts and knows your heart!

JOURNAL

Bride Behind
the Boots

Chapter Seven

DIVINE PEACE
GIVE HIM PEACE IN SURROUNDING HURT

Philippians 4:7
"And the peace of God, which transcends all understanding, will guard your hearts and your minds in Christ Jesus."

It's okay to not be okay. This is a line that I wrote in the margin of my Bible just this morning, as I sat down to write this chapter. Those words were difficult to write because I am a cheerleader, put on a smile, and "look for the best in a situation" kind of girl. When I wrote about not being okay, it was regarding the story of Queen Esther. In Esther chapter four, the queen is at a place where she is conflicted and crying, calling out to God. Sometimes we feel this way. Sometimes our husbands feel this way. Esther was going to realize that she needed to obey the unique instruction God had given her. She had to be willing to follow His call without hesitation, even with a troubled heart. It's not always the absence of fear that displays our faith and affection for God. It's when we bring it to Him and believe in the truth he proclaims over us despite our emotions. Having divine peace within our fire family lives does not mean our circumstances will be comfortable or simple.

Each moment, day, year, and season of being the wife to your fireman will take effort.

Sweet fire sister, I am here to share that difficult shift he had, or that frustrating attitude you had when he was away doesn't have to be a permanent or regular thing. Shake off the shame of feeling anxious and start new with physical peace for your body and rest for your mind in God's faithfulness. Take a big deep breath. Allow your senses to remind you of the many blessings the Lord has given you. Find a visual reminder of a peaceful time in your life. I often glance at a wedding photo that sits on my desk of my husband kissing my forehead with the sunset in the background. Listen, open your ears. *What do you hear right now?* I hear the shuffling of my toddler rolling around on the rug next to me as she has her quiet time. *What's the last thing you have eaten?* I had my favorite tea and a bowl of oatmeal this morning.

EACH *moment* *day* *year &* *season* OF BEING THE *wife* TO YOUR *fireman* WILL TAKE EFFORT

Bride Behind the Boots

What's something you can feel? I feel the keys beneath my fingers and the wrinkled pages of my Bible beside me. *What do you smell?* Honestly, I smell my husband's deodorant right now because I grabbed his out of the vanity today during my "mom morning dash," and it reminds me of him.

When my body needs physical peace and reminders, this is what I do. When I see a text about a difficult patient or just feel at the end of my rope, I try to connect the simple things around me to bring my heart back to a place of gratitude and worship. "Thank you for my wedding day, a healthy toddler, and my morning tea. By your grace, I will have gratitude and divine peace. All I need to do is ask you, God."

I've found implementing these practices when the stressors are small can help train our hearts and minds for bigger situations. It's not if the storm comes, but when the storm comes. Having Jesus within you does not grant a magical pain-free walk on this earth, but it can provide a peace that surpasses all understanding. Sometimes I will take the cause of anxiety and write it at the top of the page in a notebook. Then, I proceed to write every truth I know from God's Word that contradicts my fear. Rewire the lie for truth resulting in His assurance and peace.

Suicide calls are not something I talk about often, if ever. It's not a subject that just pops up in conversations with friends when talking about being married to a firefighter. My husband's station is zoned to take calls from the tallest bridge in Florida. The sad reality is, this bridge comes with a high amount of jumpers and suicide attempts. Sometimes, he will be at the top of the bridge with his partner and the police trying to calm jumpers' fears and convince them of the value their life holds. Once, a fellow firefighter even tackled a patient off the edge of the bridge to keep them safe. Other times, he is 430 feet below the top of the bridge on a boat administering CPR to a body that has just hit the water (Roman, 2020). My husband has shared that declaring a jumper dead and placing them in a body bag is the hardest part about being a medic. The chance of surviving is so low. However, my husband's heart aches to help and use his training to give a second chance to every patient. In this situation, that wasn't possible. These calls give me chills. After a decade of operation, this bridge has been used by over 300 people to take their lives (Aisheo, 2020). Regarding the bridge calls, I truly believe that the sweet Lord has guarded my husband's heart and mind through the peace of Jesus, like the verse at the beginning of this chapter says. I sometimes wonder how my husband does it.

Late one night, it was cold, dark, and wavy in the Gulf of Mexico. My husband's crew recovered a floating body from the water. He administered CPR as his team rushed the patient by boat to the closest ambulance. My husband's calmness through it all is something unreal. Unreal as in the supernatural. When I see his faith and trust with these situations, I know that there is a God in heaven who truly does carry and lift our burdens and fears and replaces them with His divine peace. I should not be surprised by Jesus carrying the mess because he cares for us.

PRAYER

Lord, fill my husband with your peace. Give him encouragement and rest for his weary soul and steer him away from false earthly promises for peace. When his heart feels discouraged, may he turn to you. Holy Spirit, fill me so that I may be the tool that points him back to you as the ultimate giver of true peace. If signs of stress, anxiety, or even PTSD surface in my husband's life, enlighten us to the best path forward into your freedom. Walk with us through all seasons, Lord. From the hilltops of promotions and lives saved; to the valleys of difficult calls and mounting anxiety. May we seek your presence in it all. Please help my husband's faith and trust in you bring an unending amount of peace in his career and our marriage. *Amen*

FAN INTO FLAME

Right now, quickly do the exercise that I shared earlier of connecting to your five senses. Find thanks and contentment in the things God has presently placed before you at this exact moment. If you have some quiet time to dive deep, then pluck one source of anxiety out of your brain and put it at the top of a notebook page. Shed light on it. It is not true; God's Word is true. Grab a phone or computer. Use a search engine to find a verse on the subject of the topic that is bringing you anxiety and replace the fear with truth.

For example, *Lord, I am anxious because my husband did not get an overtime shift to help pay for our bills this pay period. Truth: God will provide for us. He takes care of the birds each day; how much more does he love and care for us. Truth: God has given me a mind and hands; I can process and help develop a strategy or budget to make a practical and physical plan for this financial situation. Truth: Being in this financial position has made me more aware of you, Jesus, and how to plan or navigate this type of situation better in the future. It has helped me learn.*

JOURNAL

Bride Behind the Boots

Chapter Eight

GODLY COURAGE
LET HIM DO THE IMPOSSIBLE WITH GOD

Ephesians 6:10
"Finally, be strong in the Lord and in his mighty power."

One of my favorite quotes is, "Courage is not the absence of fear, but rather the assessment that something else is more important than fear." -Franklin D. Roosevelt. Or, in the case of a Christian's life, that "something else" is someone. God. God's will and call for a situation should always be higher than the fear. When researching the definition of courage, the one explanation that struck me pertained to how courage is having strength in the face of pain or grief. When I read those words, it tugged at my heart. This is the very reason that Godly courage is one of the most precious prayers for our men. They face the pain and grief, not merely by choice, but by being in this career. They get paid to react, treat, and serve, regardless of the danger or the suffering a patient may be experiencing. What I want to pray for are their hearts and minds.

> **May their hearts and minds be so confident in who Jesus is that courage is just a by-product of that confidence.**

Recently, my husband arrived home from a thirty-six-hour shift. It was around nine at night when he pulled into our driveway. Soon after coming inside, he was stretched out on the family room rug. I was sitting on the couch cuddling our freshly washed dog. He began to pour out, needing some encouragement to relieve the grief and pain of the past thirty-six hours. The first two calls he replayed back to me were frustrating from a medical and emotional standpoint. But the third broke me. He told me that a call came in about a sixteen-week pregnant mother who was experiencing discomfort. Upon their arrival at her home, the lifeless, tiny child had already been born. My husband shared his immediate thought in that moment of seeing the baby. "I looked down at that little life and thought, we have the same birthday." I was silent. Indeed that statement was very true, he shared a day on the calendar with that baby. My husband had worked all shift long on his birthday to meet this little life that unexpectedly was

Bride Behind
the Boots

ushered into the world the same day we celebrated him. Here we laid, on the rug and couch.

The only way we can process these heartaches on this side of eternity is to turn it back to God's goodness. From an earthly standpoint, it seemed like something bad happened that day. After sharing that he and this baby had birthdays in common, he was quick to tell me that there was somewhat of a happy ending as this little life had already met Jesus face-to-face. God knows this exact child by name. Right now, he is having the ultimate pain-free birthday party with Jesus and all the little ones in heaven. Hearing those words from my husband, that he trusts in God's mighty plan and power to have a heavenly birthday party, was a beautiful display of his courage and Godly confidence. It was the most attractive and beautiful gift he could share during that discouraging moment... truth and courage in a big God! Here on earth, in the last hour of my husband's physical birthday, in the quiet of the late-night, I finally got the opportunity to light two candles on a plate of his favorite chocolate chip cookies and sing "happy birthday." I sang to my selfless servant, as we also sang "happy birthday" with the angels to usher that other little life into heaven.

PRAYER

Lord, I pray for my husband's heart and mind concerning unhealthy fears. I pray you will keep him from questioning and keep him so very close to your mighty power and strength. Give him Godly courage to do the impossible through you. God, encourage my husband; may you give him the courage and confidence to do all that is required of him in his job. It is no coincidence that the word 'encourage' contains courage. Lord, may you be my husband's ultimate confidence. God, when needed, may you also use my words to uplift and bring life, light, and glory to your name through grief-filled calls. Thank you, Jesus, for being our hope, both now and forever. *Amen*

FAN INTO FLAME

Join me in what I call being a "word nerd." Look up the word, courage. Search definitions, scripture, and famous quotes. Read them, make a list, and process the word courage in a deeper way than you have before. When I study something deeper, I find it rests on my heart in a new and meaningful way. May your "word nerd" hunt cause the word "courage" to wash over your mind and prayers continually this week.

JOURNAL

Bride Behind
the Boots

wisdom & discernment

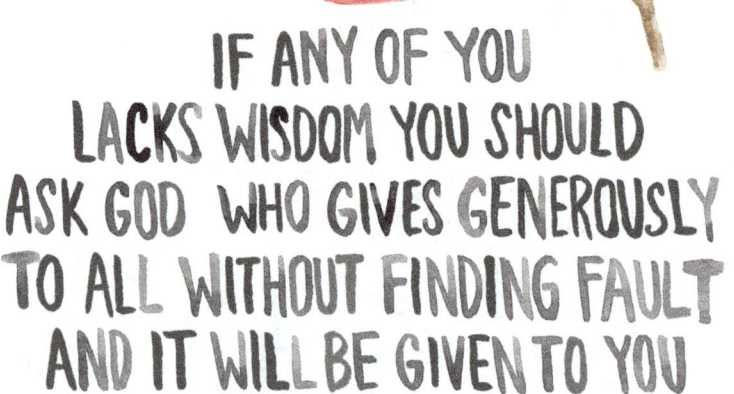

give him guidance by the Holy Spirit

IF ANY OF YOU LACKS WISDOM YOU SHOULD ASK GOD WHO GIVES GENEROUSLY TO ALL WITHOUT FINDING FAULT AND IT WILL BE GIVEN TO YOU

James 1:5

Chapter Nine

WISDOM & DISCERNMENT
GIVE HIM GUIDANCE BY THE HOLY SPIRIT

James 1:5
"If any of you lacks wisdom, you should ask God, who gives generously to all without finding fault, and it will be given to you."

We live in a world where discipline, discernment, and seeking wisdom is not always the top priority. In this fallen world, our wayward hearts seek what feels good rather than what is true. We commonly hear, "follow your heart."

Every time I hear this, I wince because the Bible tells us that the heart is deceitful above all things (Jeremiah 17:9). The only time that our hearts are to be followed is when they are in tune and aligned with the Word, the Spirit, and God's will. Hebrews 4:12 tells us that diving into His Word daily can help us "discern the thoughts and intentions of our heart."

Seeking wisdom is like dipping into a never-ending well of God's grace.

God is always gracious to give us wisdom when we seek it. We should be praying for our husbands to seek God's wisdom in every area of their lives. Whether it be spiritually, the friendships we choose, the side jobs he pursues, as well as our finances. No part of our lives is too small to seek God's truth and direction. Work is to money as income is to work. Our husbands go to the fire department and spend hours doing what is needed to bring home a paycheck. I want to take just a moment to expand on the importance of financial discernment. This is an area of passion for my husband, and one that he considers a ministry opportunity to share with others lovingly.

To provide some context in our story, we set a goal early on to support our growing family on his income only. God laid on our hearts the need for me to stay home with our little ones. I realize this may not be a goal of yours. There are so many amazing paths, careers, and family dynamics that the Lord may lead your family to. However, for me, being at home was and still is my passion… at least for now in this season while our kids are so young.

seeking wisdom IS LIKE DIPPING INTO A never ending well OF GODS grace

Bride Behind
the Boots

I don't need to tell you that relying on a paramedic's income to support a family of five takes a substantial amount of financial discipline, and a good dose of trust in God's provision. My husband's diligent planning and willingness to live without the extra things the world tells us we must have, has resulted in great peace and stability for our family. A firefighters' life is demanding enough without adding financial stress to the mix. Financial peace truly is a gift. No, our trust or stability is not in money. But, it is in a God who has given us minds to steward and care for the income we receive in a manner pleasing to him. That is our goal. To steward and glorify Him with what He gives us.

Another aspect of wisdom, I believe, is implementing guardrails. Guardrails are healthy, Biblical-based boundaries that we make in our lives to avoid temptation. Making guardrails or standards that clarify and set limits relationally, vocationaly, behaviorally, etc. can actually create peace of mind. Every guardrail is between you, your spouse, and Jesus. Mine might look different than yours. Don't be afraid to set your standards high, even if they go against the relaxed ways of this world.

Some guardrail areas to think about might be: drinking alcohol, being alone with someone who is the opposite sex (that is not your spouse), your close circle of friends who influence you the most, and the media, news, and information you put into your mind. My husband and I have seen first-hand how some of these areas have wreaked havoc in firefighter lives, because they were not guardrailed. We don't abstain or limit ourselves from these things to seem better than others who choose to participate in them. We set these guardrails because we want to protect our marriage and family for years to come. We care a lot about the things that go into our minds, because they will flow out of our hearts and mouths. Wise guardrails make life full of so much freedom. They are not restrictions but rather liberating. Knowing your standards and comfort levels ahead of time, before being put in a tough moral circumstance, liberates the mind from panic or choosing sin. Seeking wisdom should always be based on God's Word. Whether you go directly to his Word or identify mentors in areas of need, make sure you tap into resources that can guide you in honoring your Father in all you do.

PRAYER

Lord, your Word says that we simply need to come before you and open our hearts, asking for wisdom in any area. Our greatest thoughts are nothing compared to yours. May our hearts be open today for where we need to seek truth and wisdom from you. Shed light onto an area or topic in our marriage that needs more of you: faith, family, friends, finances, fire fighting, fun vacations, or food choices. Nothing is too small of a subject to apply your Word and Truth. I pray you give my husband Godly wisdom and discernment to help create stability and peace within our family unit and his department. May his heart and motives be pure. Ultimately help him to connect with you, others, and me in a deeper way as he seeks what is true and wise. *Amen*

FAN INTO FLAME

Ask God and ask another. Ask God now to nudge your heart toward an area you and/or your husband could use some guidance or wisdom. We do this about once a month. It's called the seven "F" check: Faith, Family (marriage, children, and immediate family fall under Family), Friends, Finances, Fitness/Food (health), Fire Fighting (his job), Fine Arts (my job as a painter and writer). We go through this list and rate each area on a scale of 1-10, with one meaning 'very poor' and ten indicating we rocked that topic this month. I find, oftentimes, that my husband gives me a higher score than I would have given myself… women are often our own worst critics. After we're done scoring, we brainstorm ways to improve weak performing categories. Then we pray, seeking God's direction. This process forces us to examine areas of importance to us, and identify opportunities where we can do better all while reflecting God's love.

In addition to our seven "F" process, another favorite activity is to pick up a book that speaks to the area of opportunity that I've identified. Often my book choice is a result of an online search or the recommendation of a trusted mentor. My husband has read dozens of finance and Dave Ramsey books (Ramsey Solutions, 1992). I have read many books on homemaking and child development. Find a book that encourages the topic God is nudging your heart toward today. Seek wisdom. Seek truth. Seek Him.

JOURNAL

Bride Behind the Boots

Chapter Ten

LOVE
GIVE HIM LOVE FOR HIS WIFE, FAMILY, PARTNERS, DEPARTMENT, & CHRIST

1 Corinthians 16:14
"Do everything in love."

I believe love is a choice, a process, an action, and an emotion. I also believe God is love. The divine complexity of love was given to us by our Creator. We can learn, discover, and grow in love every day. We can grow in love and intimacy with God, our spouse, and others. If you told me I'd marry a fireman before that church service, the one where I wrote on the notecard, "To be the faithful wife of a firefighter", I might have chuckled, but by God - it happened! I was attending my first college bible study one evening, and my future husband was there as well.
Honestly, I didn't even notice him as the first evening was a whirlwind of fresh new faces. Apparently, he noticed me. Later on, I learned that he mentioned to one of his firefighting buddies

that I had caught his eye. From then on, God provided many affirmations encouraging me to become more acquainted with the man who soon would be my husband. What drew me to him was his character. I fell for him because he also loved my first love, Jesus. I had begun praying for this man I didn't even know five years earlier - journaling and writing letters to him, saving my heart, emotions, and kisses for him alone.

Four short months after meeting my husband-to-be, he wrote me a letter. He quickly discovered letters were a way to this writer girl's heart. In the letter, he wrote, "I want to love you so deeply. God will always love you more.

As much as I love you, your father and mother love you; God loves you infinite times more. We can't even begin to conceive his unfailing love for us.

I am glad you have Him and have a relationship with Him. He will never forsake you and will always pick you up." Sweet fire wives, I share these little nuggets of how we met to encourage, not discourage. If your story is different, praise God because we are all on our own unique journey. Maybe neither you nor your spouse knew the Lord when you first met or got married. I share these snippets of our love story to encourage you to return to

GOD LOVES YOU
infinite times more.
WE CAN'T EVEN BEGIN TO CONCEIVE HIS
unfailing love for us.
— Caleb Lane

Bride Behind
the Boots

your first love. Not your first love of your husband, for they are human, sinful, and fail us on occasion. I'm talking about returning to the perfect love of our Savior. A safe haven of love and hope. When I need to hit the reset button on my heart, I take time to be alone with Jesus basking in His love through prayer, journaling, devotionals, reading His Word, or even a jog in the fresh air while listening to a worship song. Then, I can love others around me well, including my husband. God has given you the gift of being your husband's wife. No one else on the planet has that title. Only you. Think about that for a moment. I pray, fellow fire wives, that your love for the Almighty Creator spurs you on to love your husband abundantly.

PRAYER

Lord, thank you for your never-ending, furious love for my husband and me. Thank you that you loved us so much that you went to the cross. Fill us with more of your love and teach us to love like you do. I pray that you will give my heart a love for my husband like no one else. I thank you for the gift that he is in my life. Help me to be reminded that he is my gift and treasure when our earthly love feels strained. Take me back to more of you, Jesus. God, I will fear nothing and walk in your love today, at least at this moment here talking to you. I will mess up, but you will always forgive and love me. Teach me to have a loving and repentant heart towards you and my husband. Fill me with love. *Amen*

FAN INTO FLAME

Recall when you first came to know Jesus, when He stole your heart with His love. It's so sweet to think about, isn't it? The fresh heart feeling of amazement by a God who revealed himself to you in His perfect timing, and how He loves you so much and has shaped you since that moment. Ask Him to deepen your love for Him. Become His daughter. Each day is a new one with the choice to love Him more.

Now, recall some of the memories when you first came to know your husband. When he first stole your heart. They are a sweet reminder that he loves you, and together, you chose to walk through life as one. Lastly, since I'm a bit sentimental and romantic, do something physical to remind your husband of that first love. For example, place a wedding photograph somewhere you will both see it. One of my favorite things to do is spray the cologne that he wore on our wedding day and night in my diffuser with water. Then, when I walk into our room, the sweet aroma transports me back to our first moments and days of being married.

JOURNAL

Bride Behind the Boots

Chapter Eleven

GROWING
GIVE US MINDS TO GROW

2 Peter 3:18
"But grow in the grace and knowledge of our Lord and Savior Jesus Christ. To him be glory both now and forever! Amen."

One of my favorite quotes by Max Lucado (2020) says, "God loves you just the way you are, but He refuses to leave you that way. He wants you to be just like Jesus." I love that He refuses to leave me the same today as I was yesterday. It is a lifelong process of sanctification. Of falling more and more in love with Jesus. It will take always and forever to know Him. He is endless. Sweet fire wives, your heart to love Jesus more is my prayer for you. You have been prayed over, by me, with the writing of these pages and prayers. I pray that when you set this book down, your heart would crave more of Jesus to shape and fill you, so then in return, you can love, support, and uplift your fireman in a worthy manner. Worthy of the One who created you to be his wife. Thank you for joining me on this journey of prayer for your husband. I hope God continues to draw your heart to Him and shows you how to love in new ways. Each fire service family has its own dynamic and way of life, but let's always be reminded of Who gave us this life, each breath, and our love. Let's stay persistent in our prayers for our firefighters until our last breath, because God has gifted them to us here on this earth.

May you be your husband's best encourager, supporter, lover, and prayer warrior all the days of your life.

MAY YOU BE YOUR HUSBANDS BEST *encourager, supporter, lover, & prayer warrior* ALL THE DAYS OF YOUR LIFE

Bride Behind
the Boots

END NOTES

Aisheo, P. (2020, October 1). The Sunshine Skyway Bridge Jumper Report. The Skyway Bridge. Skywaybridge.com

Backberg, H. B. (2019, March 4). Stress: The Silent Killer of the EMS Career. EMS World. Emsworld.com/article/1222339/stress-silent-killer-ems-career

Goodreads, Inc. (2007, January 1). A quote by Franklin D. Roosevelt. Goodreads. Goodreads.com/quotes/172689

Lucado, M. (2020, August 21). Just Like Jesus. Max Lucado. Maxlucado.com/products/just-like-jesus

Ramsey Solutions. (1992, January 1). A Proven Plan for Financial Success. DaveRamsey.com

Roman, M. (2020, April 9). The Tallest, Most Impressive Bridge In Florida Can Be Found In The Community Of Terra Ceia. Only In Your State. Onlyinyourstate.com/florida/tallest-impressive-bridge-fl

ACKNOWLEDGMENTS

To the King of Kings on His Throne,
Your relentless love, redemption, and grace are what drives me. I pour out my praise and words in these pages that they might glorify you.

To My Firefighter, My Husband, My Caleb,
Without you, these pages and this process could never have unfolded. Thank you for loving and leading our family and me in ways I never knew possible.

To Jane, Clara, & Liviya,
My beautiful little curly-haired blessings.
Jane, thank you for helping mommy paint the vine in chapter six.
Clara, thank you for your innocent faith-filled prayers for Mommy.
Liviya, thank you for being my lively one-year-old through this process.
May these pages be a reflection of just how much your Mommy and Daddy love one another.

To my Mom & Dad,
Thank you for being a Godly example of loving your
spouse well through all seasons of life.
Mom, you are my rock, support, and Super Grammy.
Dad, thank you for being my editor, extraordinaire.
Thank you both for giving your blessing to Caleb when
he asked for my hand in marriage.

To Jeff & Becky,
Before asking me to be his bride, Caleb told me your love story.
His eyes were full of hope and wonder from your example. Thank
you for being Godly role models to him while growing up and to
us both today. Thank you for your help with our bubbling babies
so we could have time for our marriage and this book.

To Nana & Gub,
Thank you for being the third set of parents in my life.
You both love, support, and encourage me in everything I do.
Thank you for always pointing me back to the Savior.
Nana, the time you spent picking through my run-on sentences
will benefit everyone who opens these pages.
Thank you for the love you both poured into these words
and my life.

To Charitie,
You are my sister-in-Christ, fellow fire wife, and fellow girl mom. Your love for your firefighter paramedic and your girls truly shines as a testimony to a good God.
You carry friendship with grace and poise. Your input on these pages was as sweet as honey.

To Brent,
You made the artwork digitally beautiful beyond my abilities; thank you.

To Jodi,
An inspiration and a pure heart. God has perfectly planted you throughout different seasons of my life. From a friend, leader, coworker -for a short time-, to now, dreaming and making this book. Watching you use your God-given gifts to place all these pages and illustrations together makes my heart sing.
You are a joy to work with.

To Jess,
Thank you for using your talent to make these pages more eloquent.

ABOUT THE AUTHOR

Morgan Lane and her firefighter husband Caleb live on the west coast of Florida with their three young daughters. The passions that stir her heart are writing, painting, motherhood, and entrepreneurship. Her desire to write and paint began around the age of twelve as she began to fill journals and sketchbooks with prayers and paintings for Jesus. In 2014 she established Seaside Lane as a way to share her words, art, and motherhood journey with others in hopes to spread joy, smiles, and encouragement.

Visit her at SeasideLane.com

www.ingramcontent.com/pod-product-compliance
Lightning Source LLC
Chambersburg PA
CBHW051404290426
44108CB00015B/2152